Land and Water

by Catherine Podogil

HOUGHTON MIFFLIN   BOSTON

Landforms are kinds of land. You can
see landforms and water in many places.

Mountains

Hill

Mountains and hills are landforms.
Mountains are higher than hills.

Valley

A river flows across the land.
It may cut a deep valley. A valley is
land between hills or mountains.

Plateau

Plain

A plateau is high flat land.
A plain is low flat land.

Peninsula

Island

Land that has water
on three sides is a peninsula.
Land that has water
on all sides is an island.

Ocean

Lake

An ocean is a huge body of salt water.

A lake is a smaller body of fresh water.

7

How many of these landforms
and bodies of water have you seen?